Published in the USA by Jenny Publications

(Jennyprints.com)

email: customerservice@jennyprints.com

How to Make Wealth in a Bad Economy

-Secrets the Wealthy don't want you to Know

APPRECIATION

I want to appreciate my wife for criticizing and editing this book. Your contributions and suggestions were very helpful in this project. It is such a blessing having you as a dear friend and a helpmate who is just right for me. You are indeed irreplaceable!

TABLE OF CONTENTS

CHAPTER 1:   THE FUNDAMENTALS

CHAPTER 2:   PARADIGM SHIFT

CHAPTER 3:   THE DICHOTOMY BETWEEN THE WEALTHY AND THE POOR

CHAPTER 4:   TOUGH TIMES

CHAPTER 5:   THE ALLEGORY OF TWO FRIENDS

CHAPTER 6:   STAGGERING STATISTICS

CHAPTER 7:   THE WISDOM OF FARMERS

CHAPTER 8:   FAILURE: RAW MATERIALS FOR WEALTH

CHAPTER 9   GET MONEY FROM AN INVESTOR

CHAPTER 10: ENGAGE YOUR COMMUNITY

CHAPTER 11: WISDOM OF TIME

CHAPTER 12: START SMALL

PREFACE

It is no myth that when it comes to wealth distribution, the rich are getting richer and the poor are getting poorer. Wealth is more concentrated in the hands of the rich. However, the poor continue to languish in the misery of financial struggle and penury.

This project was born out of a very strong burden to practically unveil the secrets of the wealthy and close the inequality gap between the haves and the have-nots.

As you take interest in this project however, the purpose behind your desire to make wealth must be well defined, because if the purpose of a thing is not known, the abuse of it is inevitable.

God's reason for blessing His children is so

that they can be a blessing to others and make the world a better place. God told Abraham in Genesis 12:2

And I will make you a great nation, And I will bless you, And make your name great; And so you shall be a blessing; ...

It is also His desire that the Gospel of Christ's kingdom be spread over the surface of the earth through prosperity.

Zechariah 1:17
Cry yet, saying, Thus saith the LORD of hosts; My cities through prosperity shall yet be spread abroad; and the LORD shall yet comfort Zion, and shall yet choose Jerusalem.

It is to this end I present this project to all purpose and kingdom minded people.

Chapter 1

THE FUNDAMENTALS

The rich and poor think in very different ways, and that's the real difference between them. If you've been in a pattern of financial lack, you need to re-evaluate your financial philosophy and fine-tune it to match your goals.

The best way to determine what mental patterns are running your financial life is to look at your results, then ask yourself these revealing questions:

1. Do I consistently earn large amounts or small amounts of money? The answer to this

question is what defines and structures your budget. It sets your limits, and helps you to set your priorities. You must be in total control of your finance. Do not enter into unreasonable debt; it is a web from which many have not been able to come out. Your expenses must be far below your income. You may need to practically scale down your expenses if necessary.

2. Is my income consistent or inconsistent? This is what paints the picture of your inflow of income. The journey to financial success begins with an averagely predictable income. If your income is inconsistent, it could infer that you have some time to play it. You must begin to prayerfully think of how to make your free time productive. If you think well and look around you, there is always something financially productive you can

engage yourself and your time with. Time is the only commodity which does not discriminate. Equal amount of time is given to everybody regardless of your race, age or status. The reason many are stagnated financially is because of egotism. They feel so important that they despise certain jobs, businesses, or opportunities. If you are poor, you are poor. You need to start from somewhere in order to get anywhere in life. Don't be too arrogant to begin from ground zero.

3. Do I struggle for money or does money come easily? One of the reasons many struggle for money is simply because they chase after money. The simple way by which you create an easy flow of money into your hands is to chase after meeting the needs of your target customers, add value to yourself,

your products and services. You must sleep and wake up with this thought every day. You must intentionally build yourself up to meeting their expectations and demands. This is how to dig the well of wealth.

4. When I have money, am I an investor or a spender? Your answer to this question defines the habit you have formed. If you have formed the habit of always spending your income, you can readily predict your future; you will always remain in the class of the impoverished. Insanity is doing the same thing over and over, and expect a different result.

As an investor, do not put your eggs in one basket. Look for opportunities and avenues for diversification. This is how to be a smart investor.

5. What is the highest amount my mind has

ever let me earn? No man can ever grow beyond his mind. Proverbs 23:7 *For as a man thinks in his heart, so is he...* Your mind sets your path and creates your destination. The journey to financial freedom begins here. You must learn to build capacity for your mind by thinking out of the box.

6. Am I an employee, self employed employer, business owner or investor? According to Robert Kiyosaki, everyone belongs to either of the four quadrants below:

With this in mind, you need to answer the following question: What road-map, tailored by time-frame, do you have in crossing over to financial freedom?

7. Have I done any findings about what I want to do? Never dabble into a business you don't know anything about. It is important to do a thorough research and findings about the business or investment you want to make before investing a dime. This helps you to minimize the risk on your investment.

8. Do I have my vision and my findings written down? You must have your vision written down and rehearsed daily. It keeps you on track and sets you on the move. It creates the impetus that keeps you on your feet, and engages your mind productively.

Habakkuk 2:2:

And the LORD answered me: "Write the

vision; make it plain on tablets, so he may run who reads it.

9. Do I have the habit of procrastination? The reason many remain employed, but not deployed is because they continue to procrastinate the execution of their plans.

Procrastination is the grave in which opportunity is buried. ~Fisayo

You may delay getting started, but time will not. Be courageous and decisive enough to put a time and a deadline to getting started.

10. Am I mentally prepared to take risk?

Man accomplishes no great feat without mental preparedness. ~ Fisayo

Business ventures is generally a risk, there is no 100% success guarantee of any business ventures. However, to break free from financial paralysis, you must be willing and mentally prepared to take risk. You cannot gain much until you are willing to lose.

11. Does anybody hold me accountable for my dream?

In order to keep up with your goals, you need an accountability partner; someone that can hold you accountable and responsible for what you ought to do, and will not back off until you accomplish it. In a retreat I had with my wife some years ago, we set a five years goal for her and a timeline to accomplish it. I held her accountable on a practical note in regards to how she spent her time. Predictably, she was able to achieve the set goal in less than four years.

12. Have I defined and identified my warm market?

Identify and learn how to explore your warm market; it is a good place to lay the foundation of your business. Your initial customers are the testing ground for your business. Their feed- back is very important to help you improve on your product and services.

Chapter 2

PARADIGM SHIFT

Psalm 35:27
Let them shout for joy, and be glad, that favor my righteous cause: yea, let them say continually, Let the LORD be magnified, who has pleasure in the prosperity of his servant.

3John 1:2
Beloved, I pray that in all respects you may prosper and be in good health, just as your soul prospers.

The reason for the above scriptures is to reassure you that it is God's delight that you prosper in all areas of your life. It is unlike God to impoverish his children.

The problem with us is simply our thinking pattern and lack of financial knowledge.

Hosea 4:6

My people are destroyed for lack of knowledge

The basic difference between a wealthy man and a poor man is simply their thinking pattern.

Your thinking affects your sense of perception (how you see what you see), your perception informs your behavior, your behavior dictates your lifestyle, your lifestyle informs the inflow and outflow of resources in your life. Your thinking pattern informs your planning. It determines how you respond and take advantage of opportunities.

There is the need for a paradigm shift. Your paradigm is your subjective way of thinking. Some of the factors that influence our paradigms are: the culture of our community; our exposures; principles; values; norms; belief system; experience, education etc.

We are groomed in a culture that encourages and trains us to spend years in college with the hope and plan of getting a job after graduation. Majority of the classes and courses that are offered in institutions are mapped towards mental knowledge that does not in any way develop our entrepreneurial or investment aptitude. Towards the end of the program, the student is trained on how to write a good résumé and prepare for interview. The result is simply a mass production of employees whose opportunity in the job market has been marginalized by an increasingly emaciated economy. The effect is simply an impoverished middle class whose life's are hung on a lean and thin rope of two weeks' pay-check.

It is unfortunate that our brains are programmed for consumption. No wonder we are referred to as consumers.

In an article in the USA Today on September 17, 2013, it was confirmed that four out of 5 adults in the United States struggle with joblessness, near-poverty or reliance on welfare for at least parts of their lives, a sign of deteriorating economic security and an elusive American dream.

There is need for a radical and well informed paradigm shift, if you must remain relevant in today's economy.

Nothing is going to change for you until you change. Life doesn't get better by chance, but by practical and intentional choice to change.

You may want to know that the most powerful force God has given to man is the mind. The mind is where thought is processed. No man can ever rise above his thought. Your mind sets your limit. Your mind responds to whatever it is exposed to, and consequently influence your character/attitude and like flood, maps out a path for you.

When the prodigal son came to his senses in Luke 15:17, he made a decision that caused a turning point for the better in his life.

As you read this book, I want to encourage you to actively engage your mind and begin to write down practical and feasible decisions you have to make in the short and long run in order to eradicate poverty out of your life.

Your mind must be transformed. The mind is the place of the will. Your reactions and responses to situations and circumstances is a function of your mind. Fear, doubt, unbelief, resolutions, decisions emanate from the mind. The mind is always hungry and thirsty, therefore, the mind can be fed. The food of the mind is knowledge and information and wisdom.

If you are not financially informed, you will be economically deformed. ~Fisayo

You must be transformed by the renewing of your mind, (paradigm shift) *that ye may prove what is that good, and acceptable, and perfect, will of God.* Romans 12:2-3.

To renew means to make anew. This can only be made possible via the process of deprogramming out-of-date and out-of-touch financial information and reprogramming new and up-to-date information in your mind, such that will make you to remain relevant in the economy of this information age.

The journey of thoughts begins in the mind. Thinking creates an image, images control feelings, feelings cause actions, actions create results. If you are not getting the right financial result, you must re-examine your pattern of thinking and make the necessary change. You cannot argue against result.

New and up-to-date information can cause mind and life transformation. Learn new things!

Your mind must be equipped.

A prepared mind is guaranteed a secured future. Everything in your life today was in your mind yesterday.

Whatever your mind cannot comprehend, you hand cannot apprehend. It is your imagination that sets the pace for your destination. It is your mental picture that defines your actual future. Your thought and your future, without doubt, are in close proximity.

Seek to stay in touch with the changes taking place in the world by learning and updating your skills.

You must acquire the mental patterns that create wealth and put them to use immediately. Remember, we are creatures of habit; the habit of managing and investing your money effectively is more important than the amount you are earning today.

Chapter 3

THE DICHOTOMY BETWEEN THE RICH AND THE POOR

The basic difference between the wealthy and the poor is simply their thinking pattern.

Your thinking informs your behavior. Your behavior defines and designs your life.

Rich people work towards becoming entrepreneurs, investors and employers of labor; poor people go to school to become employees, and work to make a living.

A deteriorating lifestyle is built upon just making a living. ~Fisayo

Rich people are in control of their time, poor people's time is at the mercy of their employer. If you are ever going to graduate from the impoverished middle class, one of the key things you must be in control of is your time.

Whoever or whatever controls your time will determine your financial height.

A key step in changing your class is to be in control of yourself and your time. These are treasures you must not trade in for less than your worth.

Please ponder over this:

The best and the most productive time of the day is between 6am-5p.m. This is the time your employer engages you.

According to the Bureau of Labor Statistics, nearly 15 million Americans work a permanent night shift or regularly rotate in and out of night shifts. That means a significant sector of the nation's work force is exposed to the hazards of working nights, which include restlessness, sleepiness on the job, fatigue, decreased attention and disruption of the body's metabolic process.

Working at night runs counter to the body's natural circadian rhythm. The circadian clock is essentially a timer that lets various glands know when to release hormones and also controls mood, alertness, body temperature and other aspects of the body's daily cycle.

Our bodies and brains relax and cool down after dark and naturally spring back into action in the morning. People who work the night shift must combat their bodies' natural rest period while trying to remain alert and high functioning. It doesn't matter whether they get enough sleep during the daytime, all the sleep in the world won't make up for circadian misalignment.

Night work and fatigue may also contribute to the risk of heart disease and cancer, according to a research.

The best and the most productive season of your life is between 25-65yrs. This is the period you spend with your employers.

You must make yourself unemployable by strategically positioning yourself to become an employer of labor and a smart and active investor.

Poor people think the road to riches is paved with formal education, rich people believe in acquiring specific knowledge and skills set that is relevant to meeting the needs of their community.

People who believe their best days are behind them rarely get rich, and often struggle with unhappiness and depression. You must embrace your future by looking inward to discover your skills set, and make a concerted effort to develop them. You can never embrace the future you have not seen.

Ask yourself these questions:

i) What do I do well?

Rich people develop their skills and improve their knowledge capacity around what they do well.

ii) What do I have passion doing?

Poor people earn money doing things they don't love, rich people follow and make money from their passion.

iii) How can I create value for myself and for people who are in need of my product?

In order to answer the above questions, you must bear these three things in mind:

1. What is or are the needs of my target market? You can only get paid for meeting those needs.

2. What are my skills set in meeting these needs? If you don't have the skill set/ ability, then you must find out how you can develop yourself in that area.

3. What will be my significance in meeting the needs? Why should people prefer my products/services? Why should people come looking for my product/services? You must learn to make your product/services difficult to replace. This is where branding becomes very important.

Your significance is directly proportional to your reward. ~Fisayo

These are the three cardinals for self or product/services significance? As per your job or product/services:

Your pay will always be in direct ratio to:
i.) The need for: what you do, your product or services.

ii.) Your ability and capacity to do or provide the product/services

iii.) The degree of difficulty in replacing you or your product.

Rich people project beyond the satisfaction of self, poor people are obsessed with self.

Explanation:

Rich people engage their thought on how to engage and meet certain needs in their community using their area of strength and proficiency. Poor people are always looking forward to what their community can give them.

Don't chase after money. The Bible says, it

has wings, it will continue to elude you. *Prov. 23: 5.*

Wrap your passion around people by enhancing their lives and meeting their needs. I guarantee you, by personal experience, you will be appreciated and paid for it.

iv) How can I market myself?

Rich people are able to discover themselves, and are willing to promote and market themselves and their values. Poor people don't discover themselves, and therefore have nothing to promote and market.

It is interesting to know that technically, everyone is in the business of selling. You are either selling your product, service, skill, gift, talent, message. Generally speaking, people will first of all buy into you before buying your product. You must therefore intentionally and strategically build yourself before building your business. The quality you have developed for yourself will usually reflect in the product or services you offer.

Poor people set low expectations so they're never disappointed, rich people are up for the challenge. Psychologists and other mental health experts often advise people to set low expectations for their life to ensure they are not disappointed. No one would ever strike it rich and live their dreams without a stretch.

You don't need to do anything to fall, but you do something to rise. You don't need to do anything to fail, just do nothing

There is always a towerly cost behind every tower. ~Bishop Oyedepo.

Successful men are not lucky but worky.
~Bishop Oyedepo.

Luke 12: 49

This is serious business we're involved in. My mission is to send a purging fire on the earth! In fact, I can hardly wait to see the smoke rising. 50 I have a kind of baptism to go through, and I can't relax until My mission is accomplished!

This is where providing self-leadership becomes of paramount importance. It involves self-discipline, setting a timeline, reviewing and improving goals, developing a pattern of character tailored towards achieving your goals, holding yourself accountable for the things that engage your time. These values and principles keep you on your toes while others are sleeping, partying or watching television.

A person who cannot account for his time will in time, loose his value. ~Fisayo

Poor people believe you need money to make money. Rich people employ the power of leverage. They use other people's money and skills to make money. The rich understand how to use those who cannot build capacity for themselves to build capacity for their businesses.

You cannot accomplish significant success alone. If your vision in life is significant, you need a network of people for its fulfillment.

You cannot succeed significantly without a network of relationship. The reason God surrounds you with people is to help in the accomplishment of your goal.

The reason a self employed man will die poor stressed and broken, and his dream may not outlast him is because he does not understand and employ the law of synergy. It is the law that says you cannot do it alone.

Proverbs 27:17

Iron sharpens iron; so a man sharpens the countenance of his friend.

The truth is, you don't necessarily have to be proficient in all areas of your endeavor. You need to strategically build a network that works.

Synergy is the key to wealth. The simple path to wealth is brokerage. Always remember, there is a limit to what you can do all alone.

Poor people live beyond their means, rich people live below their means. Poor people live big and grow broke, rich people live small and grow rich.

Rich people are investors, poor people are spenders/consumers.

Pro 21:20

There is treasure to be desired and oil in the

dwelling of the wise; but a foolish man spendeth it up.

Rich people choose to get paid based on results, poor people choose to get paid based on time.

Rich people consider today as a seed to be planted for tomorrow, poor people consider today as their harvest season.

Rich people live below their means, poor people live above their means.

Rich people manage their money well, poor people mismanage their money well.

Rich people have their money work hard for them, poor people work hard for their money.

Rich people act in spite of fear. Poor people let fear stop them, so they are not willing to take risk.

Rich people constantly learn and grow. Poor

people think they already know, so they nest by their plateau.

A poor man sees the now, engages the now to meet the needs and the wants of the present, the rich man engages his tomorrow today.

Proverbs 30: 24

Four things on earth are small, yet they are extremely wise: 25 Ants are creatures of little strength, yet they store up their food in the summer;

The cash-flow pattern of a rich man revolves around, income, expenses and investment, the cash flow pattern of a poor man is income and expenses.

The Hemorrhagic cash-flow pattern of the poor

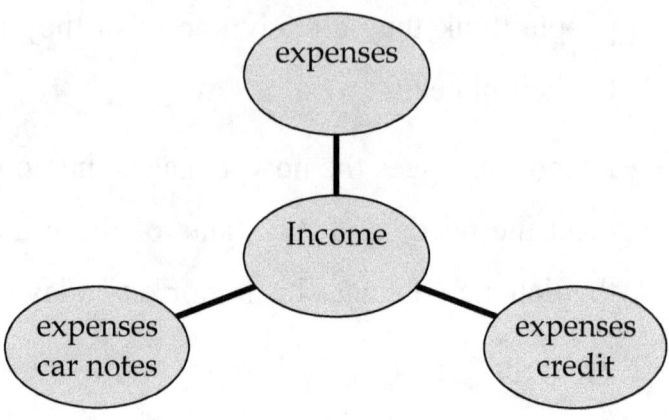

The Nourishing cash-flow pattern of the rich

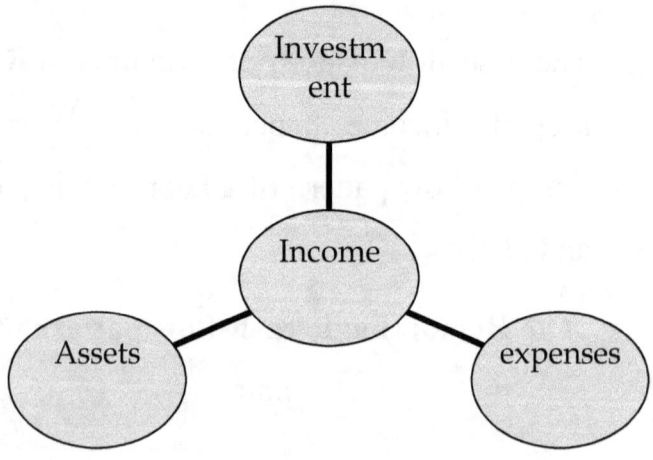

In order to be wealthy, you must understand and obey the law of sacrifice. You must be willing to sacrifice your present comfort. A seed is a sacrifice made into the earth in order to secure the future. What are you willing to sacrifice today for tomorrow?

Some of my students who were on food stamps were buying very expensive tennis shoes and name brand clothes. It sounds very ironically outlandish.

Too many people spend money they haven't earned, to buy things they don't want, to impress people they don't like. ~Will Smith

Credit cards are designed for people with this mindset.

Few list of things you must avoid buying on credit: TV, electronics, furniture, car, clothing … you can add to the list.

Rich people believe in creating and influencing their environment, the environment creates and influences poor people.

Rich people have wealth mentality, poor people have welfare mentality. The poor man believes the government, the wealthy around him or the church should be responsible for his welfare.

II Thessalonians 3:6-12,

For even when we were with you, this we commanded you, that if any would not work, neither should he eat. For we hear that there are some which walk among you disorderly, working not at all, but are busybodies. Now them that are such we command and exhort by our Lord Jesus Christ, that with quietness they work, and eat their own bread."

A man who does not take care of his own is despicable.

I Timothy 5:8,

But if any provide not for his own, and especially for those of his own house, he hath denied the faith, and is worse than an infidel.

It is about the worst indictment a man could receive to be called "worse than an infidel." It is not the government's responsibility, but a man's duty to take care of his own. Even whacked dads should be hunted down and forced to care for their own as long as they live.

Rich people have a commitment to being rich. Poor people want to be rich.

Explanation: Poor people have dreams that are not backed up by action. They have lottery and lazy man's prayer mentality.

While the poor is waiting to pick the right numbers of lottery and praying ignorantly for prosperity, the wealthy minds are thinking of meeting needs and solving problems.

Poor people pray and hope for someone to give them millions or hundreds of thousands to fulfill their dream, rich people obey the laws of wealth.

The channel of wealth is opened by obedience to the laws of prosperity, not by praying for it.
~Fisayo

Here is the simple pragmatic and unfailing biblical law of prosperity.

Gen 8:22:
While the earth remains, seedtime and harvest, cold and heat, summer and winter, day and night, shall not cease."

Rich people learn and pay the price needed to

breakthrough their plateau, poor people literarily key into status quo. The rich improve on themselves in order to remain relevant with change, poor people live in their yesterday.

Your relevance to the economy becomes nil if you are not willing to adapt to the change in the society, by educating, acquiring and updating yourself with the needed knowledge in sync with the change taking place in the society.

Consider your skill in any of these two technologies, and see how relevant you can be in today's economy.

Educate yourself by attending relevant seminars, conferences, if need be, take classes that can better equip and keep you updated in your chosen field.

Men who have no goal spend and never invest their time.

~Fisayo

Rich people are deep and productive thinkers, poor people are shallow in their thought. You are a complete sum of all your thoughts, *For as he thinks within himself, so he is.* Pro. 23:7

Rich people focus on, and take advantage of opportunities; poor people focus on obstacles.

Rich people are active investors, poor people actives spenders.

Rich people add value to their time, poor people devalue their time. Your goals define the worth of your time. Remember, time is the currency of life.

Rich people invest in their time, poor people spend their time. No wise man will invest in you, if you don't first of all invest in yourself.

Your investment in self is defined by how you invest your time. You must learn to add value to yourself by acquiring the necessary knowledge needed to help you excel in your business.

Rich people admire other rich and successful people and learn from them. Poor people resent, envy and despise the rich.

You can never attract what you resent.
~Fisayo

The law of wealth demands that you look for someone who is significantly more successful than you are, and become his protégé in order to learn strategies needed for your own success.

Rich people associate with positive, successful people. Poor people associate with negative or unsuccessful people.

Your association has a great influence over you, and can affect your thinking pattern and accelerate or impede your progress.

Proverbs 13:20:
Walk with the wise and become wise;
associate with fools and get in trouble.

Your future is predictable by the people you surround yourself with.

Rich people focus on their network and net worth, poor people focus on their working income.

Learn to think outside the box!

Chapter 4

TOUGH TIMES...

...sounds familiar?

Tough time is a very critical juncture on the path to financial success. It is an inescapable crossroad that separate the men from the boys, the poor from the rich. Your response and reaction to this season is very germane to your next level.

Rich people engage their tough times poor people build their tent around their tough times.

Life will often push you to the limits, but don't allow your emotions to get in the way. You must be strong-willed, tenacious and resilient in order to maintain your composure and actively engage your thoughts productively.

Business decisions and circumstances don't always play out logically because of several factors. Never allow the noise to stifle your thinking and decision-making capabilities. You must learn to keep a positive mental attitude as you pursue your passion. Challenges are not usually man's problem, but his reaction to them.

Challenges don't make or break a man, but reveals who he is. ~Fisayo

When you begin to fear undesirable circumstances, you not only put yourself in a position of susceptibility, but it becomes overly complex to act logically and dispassionately. When you panic, you mentally freeze and your mind loses bearing.

Decisive response to the situation at hand helps you to maintain focus and think through the situation.

Tough times never last, though people do.
Robert H. Schuller

Tough time allows the best to come out of you. Don't allow tough time to make you bitter, but better.

Poor people are full of excuses, rich people never give up.

You must develop your self confidence in order for people to believe in you. People read and buy into your conviction and self-confidence.

Rich people believe they are bigger and better than their problems. Poor people believe they are smaller than their problems.

Numbers 13: 32

So they gave out to the sons of Israel a bad report of the

land which they had spied out, saying, "The land through which we have gone, in spying it out, is a land that devours its inhabitants; and all the people whom we saw in it are men of great size. 33"There also we saw the Nephilim (the sons of Anak are part of the Nephilim); and <u>we became like grasshoppers in our own sight</u>, and so we were in their sight."

In tough times, you must be a man of passion. It is the passion you bring to your vision that helps to sustain you through the storm. Those who quit in tough time simply lack conviction and passion for what they do.

As long as you believe in who God has made you a success, you need no further conviction.

You must define your WHY in tough times. If your 'why' carries enough weight, you will garner enough strength to push through the tough time.

Use your pain to push you to greatness. If your venture is easy, every mediocre will do it.

Remember, in building a wall it is one brick at a time. Stick to the pressure and the challenge.

Never draw conclusion of defeat, there is still time to succeed for as long as you are still breathing.

When life knocks you down, you have to jump back up and yell at the top of your voice, "IT'S NOT OVER UNTIL I WIN!

A man who keeps getting back up when he's knocked down still stands a chance; he who refuses to get up looses all opportunities. You can't give up, Get back up!

Chapter 5

THE ALLEGORY OF TWO FRIENDS

The apologue of two friends who share a lot of challenges in common, but engage a different approach in addressing their challenges helps to differentiate a poor man from a rich man.

Do you have ant or grasshopper mentality?

Aesop told the fable of an ant and grasshopper who lived in the same meadow.

All summer long, the grasshopper would sing, dance and hop about, having a wonderful time. Meanwhile, the ant worked diligently, gathering and storing grain for the winter.

"Stop and talk to me," said the grasshopper.

"We can sing some songs and dance a while."

"Oh no," said the ant. "Winter is coming. I am storing up food for the winter. I think you should do the same."

"Oh, I can't be bothered," said the grasshopper. "Winter is a long time off. There is plenty of food."

So the grasshopper continued to sing, dance and hop about and the ant continued to work diligently.

Inevitably, winter came, and the grasshopper had no food and was starving. He went to the ant's house and asked, "Can I have some wheat or maybe a few kernels of corn? Without it I will starve."

"You danced last summer," said the ant. "You can continue to dance." And he closed the door without giving him any food.

Are you an ant or a grasshopper?

Are you working hard to prepare for the future, or you are living frivolously, assuming that a better future will happen by empty wishes.

Do you continue to learn, grow and develop yourself, or do you mistakenly think that today's skills will remain useful in the dynamic, ever changing world that we live in?

We must all suffer pains: the pain of discipline or the pain of regret.

~ Jim Rohn

Winter's coming and you can't avoid it, so start planning and get to work.

Ants don't sit down to continue to lament about their smallness, how insignificant they are. They simply engage their today with their tomorrow in mind. They think winter all summer. Develop and enlarge yourself when the sun is shining. Jesus said: *'I must work the works of him that sent me, while it is day: the night cometh, when no man can work'*. John 9:4

You must divide your life into phases, and put a pragmatic plan in place to start investing now.

Proverbs 6:6-11

Go to the ant, O sluggard; consider her ways, and be wise. Without having any chief, officer, or ruler, she prepares her bread in summer and gathers her food in harvest. How long will you lie there, O sluggard? When will you arise from your sleep? A little sleep, a little slumber, a little folding of the hands to rest, and poverty will come upon you like a robber, and want like an armed man.

It is ironical that the tiniest creatures are the wisest of creations. The Bible encourages that we learn from them. A quick reflection of the above scripture is important.

The period of slumbering, and procrastination is the period of inaction. The more you procrastinate, the faster poverty creeps in on you.

Ants are in the business of investing their time productively for their future, not spending and wasting it.

The ants are focused. Whatever you focus on is magnified over time. Focus leaves a mark and makes impact.

You don't belong everywhere, you belong somewhere in the economy of the universe. Seek to discover it, and commit yourself passionately and unapologetically to it until result becomes undeniably evident.

You can see your future in your focus.

Chapter 6

STAGGERING STATISTICS

Statistics about the working poor in America is overwhelmingly and embarrassingly staggering. Tens of millions of men and women struggle to get to sleep because they are stressed out about not making enough money even though they are working as hard as they possibly can. They are called "the working poor", and their numbers are absolutely exploding.

As a recent Gallup poll showed, Americans are more concerned about the economy than they are about anything else.

Why are Americans so stressed out about the

economic situation if things are supposedly getting better? Well, the truth is that unemployment is not actually going down, and the real unemployment numbers are actually much worse than what is officially being reported by the government. But unemployment is only part of the story.

Most American workers are still able to find jobs, but an increasing proportion of them are not able to make ends meet at the end of the month. The economy continues to suffer hemorrhage. Good paying middle class jobs have been outsourced, and to a large degree those jobs are being replaced by low income jobs.

Approximately 1/4 of all American workers make $10 an hour or less at this point, and we see them all around us every day. They flip our burgers, they take care of the elderly in nursing homes, they wash dishes and wait on us in the restaurants, they cut our hair and they take our money at the supermarket.

In many homes, both parents are working multiple jobs, and yet when a child gets sick or a car breaks down, they find that they don't have enough money to pay the bill. Many of these families have gone into tremendous amounts of debt in order to try to stay afloat, but once you get caught in a cycle of debt it can be incredibly difficult to break out of it. This is one of the reasons credit card is made available to people in this class.

Today, there are so many very talented American workers that are trapped in low wage work. According to the Working Poor Families Project, "About one-fourth of adults in low-income working families were employed in just eight occupations, as cashiers, cooks, health aids, janitors, maids, retail salespersons, waiters and waitresses, or drivers.

Sadly, the percentage of low paying jobs in our economy continues to increase with each passing year. This is a problem that is only going to get worse. The good paying job that you have right now could disappear at anytime and you could end up in the unemployment market very soon, if you don't put a plan in place to become an entrepreneur or an investor.

According to one survey, 76% of all Americans are now living paycheck to paycheck at least part of the time.

According to the U.S. Census Bureau, more than 146 million Americans are either "poor" or "low income" 57% of all American children live in a home that is either "poor" or "low income". About 32% of all working families were considered to be among "the working poor, even though our politicians tell us that the economy is supposedly recovering.

23.5 million U.S. children live in "working poor" homes.

In Arkansas, Mississippi and New Mexico, more than 40% all of working families are considered to be "low income". Families that have a head of household under the age of 30 have a poverty rate of 37%.

The following is a list of the most commonly held jobs in America according to the federal government. As you can see, 9 of the top 10 most commonly held occupations pay an average wage of less than $35,000 a year...

1. Retail salespersons, 4.48 million workers

earning $25,370

2. Cashiers 3.34 million workers earning $20,420

3. Food prep and serving staff, 3.02 million workers earning $18,880

4. General office clerk, 2.83 million working earning $29,990

5. Registered nurses, 2.66 million workers earning $68,910

6. Waiters and waitresses, 2.40 million workers earning $20,880

7. Customer service representatives, 2.39 million workers earning $33,370

8. Laborers, and freight and material movers, 2.28 million workers earning $26,690

9. Secretaries and admin (not legal or medical),

2.16 million workers earning $34,000

10. Janitors and cleaners (not maids), 2.10 million workers earning, $25,140.

Today, the United States actually has a higher percentage of workers doing low wage work than any other major industrialized nation does.

Median household income in the United States has fallen for four consecutive years. It dropped by a whopping $6,300 between 2001 and 2011.

The U.S. economy continues to trade good paying jobs for low paying jobs. 60 percent of the jobs lost during the last recession were mid-wage jobs, but 58 percent of the jobs created since then have been low wage jobs.

Today, more than 40% of all jobs in the United States are low income jobs.

According to the U.S. Census Bureau, the middle class is taking home a smaller share of the overall income pie than has ever been recorded before.

There are now 20.2 million Americans that spend more than half of their incomes on housing. That represents a 46 percent increase

from 2001. Low income families spend about 8.6 percent of their incomes on gasoline. Millions of working poor families in America end up taking on debt in a desperate attempt to stay afloat, but before too long they find themselves in a debt trap that they can never escape. According to a recent article in the New York Times, the average debt burden for U.S. households that earn $20,000 a year or less "more than doubled to $26,000 between 2001 and 2010".

In 1989, the debt to income ratio of the average American family was about 58 %. Today it is up to 154%.

Most people don't understand the vocabulary of debt.

According to the Federal Reserve Bank, more than 40% of American families spend more money than they earn. When the paycheck runs out, additional expenditures are often charged onto credit cards. Unfortunately, unless you receive a significant pay raise or win the lottery, it is difficult to pay these charges off, resulting in climbing balances with high interest rates.

It will take you 46 years and 1 month to pay off the balance of a $5000 credit card debt. At the end of your payment, you will have paid $13,931.11 in interest. Now, your $5000 in charges will cost you a total of $18,931.11.

In the United States today, the wealthiest one percent of all Americans have a greater net worth than the bottom 90 percent combined.

According to Forbes, the 400 wealthiest Americans have more wealth than the bottom 150 million Americans combined. The six heirs of Wal-Mart founder Sam Walton

have a net worth that is roughly equal to the bottom 30 percent of all Americans combined.

Sadly, the bottom 60 percent of all Americans own just 2.3 percent of all the financial wealth in the United States.

The average CEO now makes approximately 350 times as much as the average American worker makes.

Corporate profits as a percentage of GDP are at an all-time high. Meanwhile, wages as a percentage of GDP are near an all-time low.

Today, 40 percent of all Americans have $500 or less in savings.

The number of families in the United States living on 2 dollars a day or less more than doubled between 1996 and 2011. The number of Americans on food stamps has grown from 17 million in the year 2000 to more than 47 million today.

Back in the 1970s, about one out of every 50 Americans was on food stamps. Today, about one out of every 6 Americans is on food stamps.

More than one out of every four children in the United States is enrolled in the food stamp program.

The federal government hands out money to about 128 million Americans every single month. Federal spending on welfare has reached nearly a trillion dollars a year, and it is being projected that it will increase by another 80 percent over the next decade.

Chapter 7

THE WISDOM OF FARMERS

Proverbs 24:3-6

Through wisdom a house is built, And by understanding it is established; By knowledge the rooms are filled with all precious and pleasant riches. A wise man is strong, Yes, a man of knowledge increases strength;

The farmer is always thinking of how to turn his seed into harvest. He does not eat his seed, no matter how hungry he is, he plants it.

The seed in the hand of the farmer is what guarantees his future, he is therefore wise enough to invest and not eat it.

Identify your seed

What seed do you have that needs to be identified, cultivated, planted and nurtured into harvest?

The challenge many people have is their inability to look inward and outward and identify the seed they have and where to plant it.

Challenges of life can strip you of all you have, but not what is within you.

~Fisayo

By the law of creation, no one, animal, insects or plant on earth is without a seed. Your seed may not necessarily be money. It could be a skill that needs to be developed, a need in your environment that you must identify and engage, a connection that you have, an information you need to research on and make use of. The present challenge you have could be a seed.

Every fruit has a seed in it specifically and strategically designed for multiplication.

Your future is trapped inside of you.
~Fisayo

There is a seed in you that can eradicate poverty out of your life.

Inside the kernel of life's challenges lies life opportunities
~Fisayo

Your success is your destiny trapped inside of you. This is where your future is buried. Your future is not therefore ahead of you, but within you.

The farmer invests his seed, he does not save it. When he plants a kernel of corn, at the end of the 3rd month, it is ripe for harvest.

One ear of corn contains over 800 kernels or more. Mathematically, the farmer's returns at harvest is over 800%. There is no bank that can give you such interest on your savings.

Savings is bad, investment is good. Why? You cannot save your way to wealth. Savings can never catch up with inflation. The latest annual inflation rate for the United States is 2.1% through the 12 months ended June 2014, as published by the US government on July 22, 2014. High Yield Savings interest rate is between 0.02% to 1.% . If you do the mathematical comparison of bank's interest rate and the rate of inflation, you will discover that you are on a losing spree as you bury your money in the bank.

You must not be afraid to invest, if you must break the rules of status quo, and the back of poverty. If you stow your money in the bank, it must be between a time frame and for the purpose of active investment in a short while.

Give back.

One of the mystery of blessings is in giving. It must be part of the structures you have in place in your business to give back to God and your community, most especially, your church, your pastor and the needy.

Tithing of 10% of your profit to your local church, offering and giving to the poor is a supernatural wisdom you need to partner with

God in your business. Those who rob God of the tithe and offerings that belong to Him are living under a curse. Obviously, God always penalizes a thief. But, he always promotes and prospers the tither and those who sow seed.

Malachi 3:8,9

Will a man rob God? Yet ye have robbed me. But ye say, Wherein have we robbed thee? In tithes and offerings. Ye are cursed with a curse: for ye have robbed me, even this whole nation.

Proverbs 21:13:

Whoever shuts their ears to the cry of the poor will also cry out and not be answered.

Chapter 8

FAILURE: RAW MATERIAL FOR WEALTH

"Far better it is to dare mighty things, to win glorious triumphs even though checkered by failure, than to rank with those poor spirits who neither enjoy nor suffer much because they live in that gray twilight that knows neither victory nor defeat." Theodore Roosevelt.

As you start out on your adventure to wealth, never be afraid to fail. Failure is simply an opportunity to revisit past decisions and to devise new strategies. Persistent people begin their success where others end in failure.

"Failure is the opportunity to begin again more intelligently."

~Henry Ford

Let's glean wisdom as we learn from those who were able to cross the borderline of the average when it comes to the economy of money.

WALT DISNEY

Before Walt Disney built the empire he has today, he was fired by a newspaper editor because "he lacked imagination and had no good ideas."

In 1921, Walt formed his first animation company in Kansas City, where he made a deal with a distribution company in New York, in which he would ship them his cartoons and get paid six months down the road. He was forced to dissolve his company and at one point could not pay his rent and reportedly survived by eating dog food.

Also, When Walt first tried to get MGM studios to distribute Mickey Mouse in 1927, he was told that the idea would never work because a giant mouse on the screen would terrify women.

Entrepreneur Walt had a whole slew of bad ideas before coming up with good ones.

"Success is going from failure to failure without losing your enthusiasm." Sir Winston Churchill

OPRAH WINFREY

At age of 22, the now-TV mogul was fired from her job as a television reporter because she was "unfit for TV."

Winfrey was terminated from her post as co-anchor of the 6 o'clock weekday news on

Baltimore's WJZ-TV after the show received low ratings. Winfrey has called it the "first and worst failure of her TV career." She was then demoted to morning TV, where she found her voice and met fellow newbie Gayle King, who would one day become her producer and editor of O, The Oprah Magazine.

Seven years later, Winfrey moved to Chicago, where her self-titled talk show went on to dominate daytime TV for 25 years, and ultimately head her own channel, OWN.

"Many people dream of success. To me, success can only be achieved through repeated failure and introspection." Soichiro Honda

THOMAS EDISON

When Thomas Edison was seeking to invent

the electric light bulb, he didn't get it right the first time. Did he immediately throw a 'wobbly' and say, "I'm a big fat failure!"? Did he throw his arms up in the air and sigh, "This is just too hard. I give up!"?

When it didn't work the first time, Edison made a note of exactly what he'd done and what components he had used. Then he made an adjustment to the experiment and tried again.

And when that "failed" he made a note of that, modified and tried again. He kept learning from every experiment. He learned all the ways that it wouldn't work. He discovered all the chemicals and elements that wouldn't work. And each time he found a way that wouldn't work, he knew he was closer to finding a way that would work.

It took him approximately 10,000 experiments

to invent the perfect set-up for the electric light bulb. There was a lot of learning to go through. Nobody had done it before. He couldn't read a book about it. He simply had to plug away, failing and learning, until he and his muckers worked out the right way to do it.

"If you have made mistakes there is always another chance for you - you may have a fresh start any moment you choose, for this thing we call 'Failure' is not the falling down, but the staying down."

~Mary Pickford

SIDNEY POITIER

Sidney Poitier was told to become a dishwasher.

After his first audition, Poitier, who grew up poor in the Bahamas, was told by the casting director, "Why don't you stop wasting people's time and go out and become a dishwasher or something?"

Poitier went on to win an Oscar for "Lilies of the Field" in 1964 and 1967's super successful "Guess Who's Coming To Dinner."

"If you don't accept failure as a possibility, you don't set high goals, you don't branch out, you don't try - you don't take the risk." -

~Rosalynn Carter

MICHAEL JORDAN

Michael Jordan was cut from his high school basketball team. A young Michael Jordan went home and cried in the privacy of his bedroom. But Jordan didn't let this early-in-life setback stop him from playing the game and the basketball superstar has stated, "I have missed more than 9,000 shots in my career. I have lost almost 300 games. On 26 occasions I have been entrusted to take the game winning shot, and I missed. I have failed over and over and over again in my life. And that is why I succeed."

"I've never been afraid to fail. Michael Jordan

STEVE JOBS

Steve Jobs was removed from the company he started. He was a college dropout, a fired tech executive and an unsuccessful businessman. At 30-years-old he was left devastated after being unceremoniously removed from the company he founded.

In a 2005 commencement speech at Stanford University, Jobs explained, "I didn't see it then, but it turned out that getting fired from Apple was the best thing that could have ever happened to me. The heaviness of being successful was replaced by the lightness of being a beginner again, less sure about everything. It freed me to enter one of the most creative periods of my life."

After his return to Apple, Jobs created several iconic products, including the iPod, iPhone and iPad, which have changed the face of consumer technology forever. He became one of the richest men in the world.

"An inventor fails 999 times, and if he succeeds once, he's in. He treats his failures simply as practice shots."

ELVIS PRESLEY

In 1954, Elvis was still a no-name performer, and Jimmy Denny, manager of the Grand Ole Opry, fired Elvis Presley after just one performance telling him, "You ain't goin' nowhere, son. You ought to go back to drivin' a truck."

Elvis went on to become the second best-selling artists of all time.

"When I was a young man, I observed that than nine out of ten things I did were failures. I didn't want to be a failure, so I did ten times more work " George Bernard Shaw

ABRAHAM LINCOLN

A list of the failures of Abraham Lincoln

- 1831 - Lost his job

- 1832 - Defeated in run for Illinois State Legislature

- 1833 – He ailed in business

- 1835 – His sweetheart died

- 1836 – He had nervous breakdown

- 1838 – He was defeated in run for Illinois House Speaker

- 1843 – he was defeated in run for nomination for U.S. Congress
- 1848 – He lost re-nomination to congress
- 1849 – He was rejected for land officer position
- 1854 – He was defeated in run for U.S. Senate
- 1856 – He was defeated in run for nomination for Vice President
- 1858 – He was again defeated in run for U.S. Senate
- 1860 – He was elected the President of the United States of America.

That looks like a pretty glum résumé, making you wonder how he ever made it to the top.

You first learnt to walk after falling down thousands of times. Thank God you didn't take every fall as some personal flaw - or you'd still be riding around in a buggy!

"Failure is an event, never a person; an attitude, not an outcome." Zig Ziglar.

Chapter 9

HOW TO GET MONEY FROM AN INVESTOR

Many people often complain that the reason they could not start a business is because they do not have the capital to start the business of their dream. So, they continue to wait hopelessly for the right time.

What you need to start up your business or investment is an idea. There are multiplied millions of people who have money they are willing to invest, but lack idea. Such people can become the leverage you need to get you started if you are able to come up with a sound business idea.

A lot of people out there lock up their money in savings account. They are not willing to venture out and actively engage in investment simply because they don't know how.

From experience, there are warm investors around you who are watching how you are going about your business. They will be willing to invest in it without much persuasion, if you have credibility of industry, integrity of character and time-tested result of the little you are doing.

Luke 16:10:
"Whoever can be trusted with very little can also be trusted with much, and whoever is dishonest with very little will also be dishonest with much.

In order to come up with a sound business idea that will convince an investor, you must be willing to do a thorough research and practical findings about your business. It must factor in your strength and acumen. It must be relevant to the basic needs of the target consumer; the advantages of the business proposal must be highlighted.

You must have a well stated startup budget. You must highlight convincing profit opportunities for the investors. You must have a timeline for the growth of your business; every business plan ought to include tasks, deadlines, dates, forecasts, budgets, and metrics. It must be measurable.

Be very specific and pointed in your proposal. You must state in a categorical and factual sense, based on your conservative projection, the percentage of the commission of the investors. It must be convincing and reasonable.

An investor wants to know how much you are willing to or have already committed to the business. Wisdom tells an investor how unserious you are, if you have been working for x number of years, and you have not been able to save up anything as a starting capital.

I was going to start a business sometimes ago, as I approached investors, they wanted to know how much I was willing to commit to the business myself. My bank statement was a proof of my readiness to start the business. This helped me to get three times of my initial capital to get the business started.

Get the investor fascinated and committed. The definition of commitment to an investor: in a bacon and egg breakfast, the chicken is involved, and the pig is committed.

An average investor is majorly concerned about his returns. Your proposal must therefore make sense, and sound convincing enough to him.

This is why you must sit down and do thorough homework and house-keeping before you approach an investor.

Allow couple of trusted parties to help review your proposal, quiz and criticize it. In doing this, be careful of pessimists.

Caution:

It is always a best practice to start up your idea with the little you have. You don't want to start your business or investment with debt for these reasons:

By experience, it puts a lot of pressure on you. You will start paying commission almost the following month of starting up your business. Most businesses don't mature until after one year. By that time, you must have experimented and gained a lot of experience that can help sustain your business or investment.

Business is a risk, and you have the tendency of not getting it right the first and second time. You don't want to lose your credibility before the investors, you may need them in the nearest future.

Chapter 10

ENGAGE YOUR COMMUNITY

Learn to engage your community by identifying the need of the people in it. People have needs for which they are willing to use money to solve. Where there are needs and problems, there are opportunities.

People who make money start out to solve problems and meet needs. They don't start out to make money. It is in being diligent, focused and intentional about their pursuit that they start making money.

You must develop a very positive attitude to life and towards people. Your attitude determines who are attracted to you. If you have a negative attitude, you will attract negative people, if you have a positive attitude, you will attract positive people. The community generally responds to positive and caring people.

In engaging your community, you have to define your target customers. It is important to do some research about the population of your target customers. It must involve the following:

i) Who are your target customers?

ii) What are their needs you intend to meet?

iii.) How important are the needs to them?

iii) Are your products or services affordable?

iv) Who are your competitors in the business?

v) What makes you different from them? Why

should your customers prefer your services/products? What makes you stand out?

You must consider how your product will differ from others, and why yours should become the product of choice in terms of price, quality, delivery, etc.

Strategic advertisement:

Branding:

The American Marketing Association (AMA) defines a brand as a "name, term, sign, symbol or design, or a combination of them intended to identify the goods and services of one seller or group of sellers and to differentiate them from those of other sellers.

Therefore it makes sense to understand that branding is not about getting your target market to choose you over the competition, but it is about getting your prospects to see you as the only one that provides a solution to their problem.

The objectives that a good brand will achieve include:

- Delivers the message clearly
- Confirms your credibility
- Connects your target prospects emotionally
- Motivates the buyer
- Concretes User Loyalty

In order to succeed in branding, you must understand the needs and wants of your customers and prospects. You do this by integrating your brand strategies through your company at every point of public contact.

Your brand resides within the hearts and minds of customers, clients, and prospects. It is the sum total of their experiences and perceptions about you and your product. I read earlier today about Mercedes-Benz branding: 'The best or nothing'. Toyota: 'World's most valuable car.' My graphic design company brand is: 'The zenith of creativity'

It's important to spend time investing in researching, defining, and building your brand. After all, your brand is the source of a promise to your consumer. It's a foundational piece in your marketing communication and one you do not want to be without.

The power of your brand relies on the ability to focus. That is why defining your target market will help to strengthen your brand's effectiveness.

Put your products in the faces of your target customers. In this information age, the internet is a good source of marketing your products and services. Take advantage of the social media. Deliberately enlist business/services in a social media site, search your target market and continue to add them on your friends list.

Use this medium as a platform for advertisement.

You must continue to put your products and or services in the face of your customers in every way possible.

Capacity and credibility are the keys to building a good business.

Chapter 11

THE WISDOM OF TIME

Time is the currency of life. Time is exchanged for your worth.

How do you know your worth? Pay attention to what engages your time.

~Fisayo

Your time and your value is a trade by barter. Time is critical to your sense of significance. Whoever takes your time has your life. because it is a portion of your life.

Psalm 90:12

So teach us to number our days that we may get a heart of wisdom.

Your worth is defined by what occupies your

time
. ~Fisayo.

If you can control what occupies your time, you can influence your worth.
~Fisayo

What you are paid is defined by how your employer defines your worth
~Fisayo

How much do you sell your time?

If you are not happy with your pay, intentionally engage your time with what is more productive
~Fisayo

When man defines your worth, they cheapen your value
~Fisayo

Your goal defines the worth of your time.

Men who have no goal spend and never invest their time.
~Fisayo

Anything you don't have is what you have been unwilling to exchange for your time.

You are only competing with yourself and time, this is why you must place value on your time.

Ecclesiastes 3:1-2

1 For everything there is a season, and a time for every matter under heaven: [2] a time to be born, and a time to die; a time to plant, and a time to pluck up what is planted;

Put a value on your time! You cannot place value on your time until you set goals with deadlines, and you are willing to hold yourself and be held accountable.

The reason God gives you time is to enable you fulfill your purpose.

Genesis 8:22

[22] While the earth remains, seedtime and harvest, cold and heat, summer and winter, day and night, shall not cease.

Be careful of time wasters.

Those who squander your time obliterate your enterprise.

~Fisayo

If you can't plan a day, a week, a month, a year, how can you plan your life?

The most effective way of managing your time is by setting your priorities. Steven Covey, the renown American educator, author, businessman, and keynote speaker, explained setting priority with this metaphorical illustration:

One day this expert was speaking to a group of business students and, to drive home a point, used an illustration.

As this man stood in front of the group of high-powered over-achievers, he said, "Okay, time for a quiz." Then he pulled out a one-gallon, wide-mouthed mason jar and set it on a table in front of him. Then he produced about a dozen fist-sized rocks and carefully placed them, one at a time, into the jar.

When the jar was filled to the top and no more rocks would fit inside, he asked, "Is this jar full?" Everyone in the class said, "Yes." Then he said, "Really?" He reached under the table and pulled out a bucket of gravel. Then he dumped some gravel in and shook the jar causing pieces of gravel to work themselves down into the spaces between the big rocks.

Then he smiled and asked the group once more, "Is the jar full?" By this time the class was onto him. "Probably not," one of them answered. "Good!" he replied. And he reached under the table and brought out a bucket of sand. He started dumping the sand in and it went into all the spaces left between the rocks and the gravel. Once more he asked the question, "Is this jar full?"

"No!" the class shouted. Once again he said, "Good!" Then he grabbed a pitcher of water and began to pour it in until the jar was filled to the brim. Then he looked up at the class and asked, "What is the point of this illustration?"

One eager beaver raised his hand and said, "The point is, no matter how full your schedule is, if you try really hard, you can always fit some more things into it!"

"No," the speaker replied, "that's not the point. The truth this illustration teaches us is:

If you don't put the big rocks in first, you'll never get them in at all."

What are the big rocks in your life? A project that you want to accomplish? Time with your loved ones? Your faith, your education, your finances? A cause? Teaching or mentoring others? Remember to put these Big Rocks in first or you'll never get them in at all.

Chapter 12

START SMALL

It is always wise to start small. Learn to take baby steps initially. It is wisdom for life. You were once very insignificant in your mother's womb, see how tall and big you are today.

Zech.4:10

Do not despise these small beginnings, for the Lord rejoices to see the work begin,

Job 8:7

Though your beginning was small, Yet your latter end would increase abundantly.

The reason many are not able to venture out into the business world is because they believe they don't have enough capital to start business.

You can actually start a business with little or no capital. I started a business with N1,600 naira which is equal to $10 when I was an undergraduate. Within a year, I was able to buy a car, rented an apartment and paid my way out of college.

Be a broker

A broker is an individual or party (brokerage firm) that arranges transactions between a buyer and a seller for a commission when the deal is executed. A broker who also acts as a seller or as a buyer becomes a principal party to the deal. I have made some money doing this.

This is the best way to start a business without capital. A good business man is a man who is able to explore and translate his ideas into money.

If you have any business in mind, there is a tendency that other people around are doing similar business. You can start by being a broker. Some of them may be willing to enroll you into their reseller program. You simply get the job and outsource it.

In satisfying a customer or client, the job must be done right and on time. Who, and where the job is done is secondary to the customer.

Note that your business secret is your strength in the business.

Don't tie your capital down by buying equipment.

Depending on the type of product or services you want to start, equipments can be very expensive. It is not usually wise to use your capital in buying equipment. I got burned making this mistake.

However, you can lease equipment or produce your product by liaising with people who already have the equipment. You can agree on terms with them to pay a certain amount or percentage of the product for using their equipment.

Start with your tax refund

For those in the western world, consider starting your business with your tax refund. The big screen TV, or the latest phone can wait.

Do a thorough research about the business you are about to start, and take wise counsel before you start anything. Endeavor to put your plan in place, do your homework and housekeeping before you receive the check.

Cut your frivolous expenses. Learn to make do with basic needs. Don't live big yet. Lay low, and be strategic.

Consider your first real estate as your initial investment

Your home with a 30years mortgage is definitely a liability, and not an investment.

You can make your first home as your first investment. Stay in an average apartment while you buy a foreclosed home in a prime neighborhood. Renovate and lease it out. You can consult a leasing company to help you lease it. You need to come up with another investment opportunity where the extra income from your first investment is systematically and strategically diverted.

Another option is to buy a house that has a ready to move in basement or that needs renovation that is within your budget. You can lease it out to a tenant. Do a criminal background check for the prospective tenant. It is wise to involve an attorney in the process.

Few factors you must consider as you venture into real estate investment:

1. The monthly rental fees must be strategically set aside to either pay off your house in less than 10 years.

2. You may want to consider diversification

3. Be careful of incurring debt for renovation.

4. Make sure your real estate is within bus route for easy mobility for someone who doesn't have a car.

Agriculture:

Agriculture is a time proven business venture that has yielded great returns for so many investors. It is a recession-proof business.

You may need to synergize with a very reliable and credible partner if you are embarking on this project abroad. If you do it right, you will definitely make profits or ongoing returns for your investment.

Large Scale Farming: Beans Plantation,, Cassava plantation, Palm tree Plantation, Tomato Plantation, fishery, poultry.

Small Scale Food Processing: Soya Processing Small Plant: Soy Milk, Tofu and Yogurt , Cassava Processing Plant, Rice Mill, Maize and Sorghum Milling, Maize Processing Plant, Palm Oil Extraction Mill

Catering and Bakery: Restaurant, Pizza Parlor Bakery. If you have passion for cooking, you can learn how to prepare these types of foods on the internet, most especially, on YouTube.

Locate a community of people who are in

need of your products; identify your competitors and come up with a unique way to compete with them. You can decide to do a mobile restaurant. You may need to get a license to do this type of business.

The internet has made the world a global village. There are multiplied number of web business opportunities springing up by the day. There are many people whose web stores like eBay, Amazon, Craigslist and many others have fetched them multiplied thousands of dollars. I needed to buy two cars for my children the other day; I went on online to locate a seller. I ended up buying two cars from an individual seller. I will strongly encourage for you to do a thorough studies and research on how to market your products and services on the web.

In closing, I pray that the God of our Lord

Jesus Christ, the Father of glory, may give to you a spirit of wisdom and of revelation in the knowledge of Him. I pray that the eyes of your heart may be enlightened, so that you will know what is the hope of His calling, what are the riches of the glory of His inheritance in the saints, and what is the surpassing greatness of His power toward us who believe.

See you at the top!

OTHER BOOK WRITTEN BY THE AUTHOR:

OTHER BOOK WRITTEN BY THE AUTHOR:

COMING OUT SOON

www.ingramcontent.com/pod-product-compliance
Lightning Source LLC
Chambersburg PA
CBHW051547170526
45165CB00002B/920